LEFT
ON
READ

COPYRIGHT

Ordering Information:

Visit my website:
http://www.matthewcalderwood.com

Quantity sales. Special discounts are available on quantity purchases by corporations, associations, and others. For details, contact the publisher.

TABLE OF CONTENTS

FOREWARD

Woohoo. You are reading the section of the book that almost no one reads. Thanks. The fading interest in reading has caused me to wonder whether books and literary art will one day be cast aside. I feel that writing is a way for individuals to be able to express themselves. This is my expression. I continue to write many of these poems through a problem-solving lens and in no way advocate for anyone to partake in self harm, underage drinking, drug use, or any harmful behavior towards ones self or others.

Quite the opposite! Writing is my outlet and is a way for me to be expressive. I encourage others to pursue a form of art that allows for their expressive nature to communicate. I also encourage you to read this book because I believe that it will help you.

If you are feeling distressed or suicidal, please reach out to someone. Society is awful but it isn't so bad when people like you and me get to talk. If you are in an emergency concerning your mental health:

Call 1-800-784-2433 or 1-800-273-8255 in the United States!

If you are just looking to talk, contact me via my website!

DEDICATION

*I dedicate this book to my Lord and Savior Jesus Christ,
my mom and dad,
Maggie, Tyler, Michael, Noah, Abigail, and Elijah.*

If you are feeling distressed or suicidal, please reach out to someone. Society is awful but it isn't so bad when people like you and me get to talk. If you are in an emergency concerning your mental health:

Call 1-800-784-2433 or 1-800-273-8255.

CHAPTER 1
LOVE

What is true αγάπη?

Imagine to yourself, life being entirely different. Have you ever tried to imagine love? I've always had trouble with that. Perceptions of what love is unfortunately is regularly twisted. Worthy of note, this is often not our fault. Society looks to diminish humanities finest purpose to steal resources, potential, and purpose from all of us. I believe education about love is something that we must experience before we can go about eliminating the mistreatment.

I prefer my made up, biased, personal, definition of the word love:

An emotion created by the passion between two people of whom will not only lay down their lives for each other but also would do anything to see the other for one more fleeting moment. The feeling creates butterflies or a overwhelming excitement both the first moment and every time they see each other. Every time their eyes connect they experience this feeling. It is neither a noun, a verb, or an adjective but a combination of the three. Love is beautiful, kind, and joyful. Love is a bond, forged in pain not won through success. Paid for not stolen. One can not simply "steal a heart" to gain love... it must be given to them. Love is when deep down inside you know you would never be the same without the other person. Love is built. Love is fought for. Every choice you make affects its condition. Life is not life without it but pain is not severe without it as well.

3

I believe this definition eliminates nearly all the "I love you" statements we have said in the past. Society has realigned us onto a path of self destruction by creating a culture of easy love. Love and charity are not the same. Society erodes are resolve and fights to break us down. We are not "pretty enough" without make up. We are not as strong as we should be. Sex is okay when we want to keep a relationship. Society is a liar. They want you to give them your resources: time, energy, happiness.

I propose we stop this

People walk around hushing each other if they say swear words and yet won't caution against abuse of some of our most important words. They don't understand this emotion. Explain it to them. Listen to their thoughts. Share what love really is by discussion not via lecture. Fight for love, don't settle for the watered down version.

;

Following a conversation with a friend I finally
discovered what this illusive symbol was
designed to mean

;

"When the sentence ends but the thought
continues"

My sentence ended but my thoughts still
continue,

it's like after you order and there is something
WAY better on the menu,

it's a representation of all the valentines that I
meant to send you,

We are separate now, but I crave to put the
sentences together,

I thought about a ton of commas but that
would never,

work out because the sentences would be
severed,

by a pause that is just uncomfortable,

leaving the thought vulnerable,

Maybe if I write some lovey-dovey poetry you
might want to connect,

I could just enchant myself instead of being
direct,

Write about the blissful experience of being
drawn in by your gaze,

But honestly I'm still hung up on a certain
summer day

A day full of thoughts where the sentences
were there to add,

A day full of shots where the memories were of
my dad,

But you still found a way to be comforting,

I kept running and you would still come to me,

Even if I obsess over basic poetic words
instead of writing how I feel,

That obsession just attempts to conceal my
real thoughts of which I am trying to heal,

I'll refrain from looking to the calendar and remembering certain days,

I'll attempt to not sound so depressed somehow or someway,

{ but }

The enchantments, the bliss, the gazing aside,

I'd rather be with you tonight; just you and I

...I and you...

...because even if I end, I want us to continue...

I'D LIKE TO BE YOUR WHISKEY

There is a type of shiver that runs down your spine when you take your first shot

Similar to the time I first really caught your eyes...

Obviously we were young the very first time...

it didn't make a whole lot of sense and we just lived our lives

but I feel like if we had that real moment now we would be a lot better off.

I hate having to wait for the inevitable pain to strike.

(H8 with an 8 cause I know that just isn't "right")

I hate starting sentences with "I" or being to basic.

I feel like every time I start a rhyme it just ends up wasted.

As though it could've been done better, wow.
Isn't that the story of my life?

We have a lot more in common than you think,
but sure you can fight?

We can complain, get pushy, I can sleep on the
couch for a fortnight

Scratch and claw your way into my mind, I
guess you can keep trying to make yourself
worthless,

Won't change my immediate response from
being "nah, you're perfect"

Let's be real. None of us are. (Sorry, but we
established, I am a liar a long while ago.)

I'll recite to you poems and talk of desires for
hot chocolates and fires

I want to be around when you pick your inner circles

I want to be the blue with you, one day, maybe make purple?

You always told me you were a drinker, called me a brave thinker,

I could never figure out if that was an insult to my spirit or my figure,

I chased after you, I attempted to be the perfect fit,

I was a lite beverage, you wanted whiskey, and I only had sobriety and wit,

Wow... this is getting cliché.

Whatever, it gets like this every day, I daydream, life dream, I'm obscene? I get it.

My life is becoming just a giant poetic message:

WHAT NOT TO DO!: A Life Story of Myself

Seems like a pretty accurate representation of
every time I try to talk to someone and then it
just all ends poorly and I just don't know how
to interact and make you like me, my mind is all
fuzzy, this writing doesn't make sense and that
is so funny because the only thing that has
ever... was vodka and you.

But the vodka hurts and I'd rather be your
whiskey.

THERE IS THIS FEELING

There is this feeling. This one that I have every time I look in your eyes.

It's something that if I am not looking first it catches me by surprise,

no matter how many times I experience it I still

realize that no prescription could ever give me something like this high.

Honestly it gets awfully cliché in my writing style, I admit that I write certain sentences to make you smile. I will never be ashamed of the fact that your expression of happiness however fleeting makes my brain go wild.

The feeling that I find myself writing about all the time, well it's something that is always on my mind. I always find that it can take me from fine to one of a kind while not having me only being able to say one word at a time.

Because

I.

Love.

You.

I say while I gasp for air each time our lips part,
I speak from my innermost feelings of my heart
and I have felt these feelings since the start.

I know I could last for days underwater with
just you and I exchanging oxygen. Transferring
breath, the warmth of your body, I always find
myself talking.

But then again, I do not. Sometimes I find
myself breathless, mesmerized, desiring to get
caught up in your arms, with them wrapped
around my neck running your fingers through
my hair and tying our tongues in knots.

I want to shout about how much I love you
when you worry so that you feel more safe, but
sometimes geographically we are not always in
the same place. So to replace the tragic case
that we are not face to face.

Picture us, you worried like you may be now. Sitting down focusing on all the thoughts gathering like a crowd. Then imagine me wrapping my arms around your waist and making silly jokes hoping to make one count.

Instead of shouting I just move slowly to your ear, whispering just loud enough for it to be clear. I love you hun, is what you would hear while I try to make all the worries disappear.

Yet, I am the one that gets the most out of our interaction. Your pleasure is something I crave.

TIME ENOUGH

Fluttering always seemed like an interesting word to me,

It seemed like something you could only experience when you were free or happy,

But it is the only way I could describe this feeling... you'll see,

Two lovers dance across the petals of a flower and waltz through the skies draped with white lace,

The dance looks like one of the lovers is in constant chase,

But in reality each is circling the other, they take turns chasing each other,

their satin wings occasionally brushing against their lovers, until the moon rises and they go back to their flower petal covers,

Tomorrow will be another dance, tomorrow they will return to the blue dance floor,

Their relationship has always been one that is passion and love at its core,

The hearts of butterflies beautifully beat in the belief that life isn't much, Butterflies don't count their lives by months but moments and they believe they have time enough,

We as people seem to always go through a metamorphosis of our own,

Like its required to change from the old to finally be grown,

The two lovers realize they are lucky they are not alone,

That they have someone that they can return with to their home,

The sun rises and falls many times and they dance together with smiles in their hearts,

Butterflies in their stomachs at the slightest touch they never wanted to part,

From the skies to the leaves, the little couple could even be found waltzing through trees,

They finish their days dance and went back to their flower petal beds,

To lay down their little heads,

Tomorrow will be another dance, tomorrow they will return to the blue dance floor,

They were lying awake thinking about each other, longing to dance once more,

Slowly but surely their lives were reaching the end of their forever,

But they still danced together not caring about the weather,

Rain or sunshine it didn't matter to them they just continued to float through the air,

Looking in each others eyes they didn't chase anymore they just remained close and in each others care,

Their love was a fluttering profound love, one that in their hearts always felt like enough,

The final days ended for the two lovers and so they went back to their flower petal covers,

One of the lovers knocks on the petal door, he wants to know if his lover will have one dance more on the starry dance floor,

And even though their legs felt weaker, and their wings felt heavier,

They still felt joy and love at the end of their forever,

Wings beating against the midnight breeze,

they smile looking in each others eyes not ever wanting to leave,

And even though tomorrow won't be another dance and they won't return to the dance floor they will still be okay,

because love like theirs can never decay,

The final day came to a close and the two lovers went back to the same flower petal covers,

Arm touching arm and wings brushing against wings their last breaths were with each other,

And even though their bodies will be lost their love never will,

because they truly had time enough during the dances when time stood still,

A FLAME

A simple murmur of fire. A glowing piece of
life and death. Destruction and order within
a single body of glowing red and orange. It
is no wonder why we refer to passion in a
relationship to be a fire. We crave the warmth
that can only be provided by another body.
Another soul. I wish to be near you, to absorb
your scorching kiss. Leave burn marks on my
body but let my spirit feel your entirety. I know
this love is lethal but if I am going to leave this
world I want to go in a fire work of combustion.
An explosion that all the passerby. Burn. Burn.
Burn my skin. I'm caught in the mesmerizing
control of the flickering flames flying through
the air. I fear the cold because that means
that I am not with you or we are not the same
which in my mind is worse. I know that if I were
cold and alone the scars from this scorching
interaction would leave enough warmth inside
me.

Like a candle in the wind, this flame starts off delicate and easily able to be snuffed out. As it grows and the wax melts the fire expands. Oh, how noticeably gorgeous it truly is. You are but the flame to my life and without you it would be cold and dark. No light to be guided by. Some would control you placing walls between you and their hands. Some would try to control you and use you to do their bidding. Not me. I just wanted your love until I burned out. I didn't realize that if we were the perfect match and we caught fire we would flake away and die. I am all used up, honestly just pathetic and yet you are so beautiful and amazing... I understand I can't ever deserve the warmth of the flames but can't a man be understood. I wish my thoughts would stop because all I can think about is you, your protection, and our fire.

FOR THE LOVE OF GOD

You like to cast judgement. Shut up, you do.

My unrhymed, unfiltered mind, wanted you to,

I inhaled the chemicals, poured blood on the
soil,

Embraced the chaser, sought after more
turmoil,

I craved the feeling of losing control,

In pre-written futures is where I look for my
soul,

You scoff at my misfortune mistaking privilege
for a goal,

I wince at reinforcement, resting memories of
the pole

This is an amusement park life, more like a
bruising park life,

The cotton candy with history of enslavement
and not a single fun ride,

But you like to cast judgment, tell me I am
doing it all wrong,

Tell me I messed up, shouldn't do that, while
blaring a song,

I want to be pretty, perfect teeth, and
astonishing eyes,

Funny, how the pretty people always end up
being those who died, ... and I am always alive

I want to be someone who you can at least like,

You reach to be friends with me in this hole I
dug and within I hide

My grandfather was one who could feel the
weather change in his bones,

I can't weather your disgust all on my own,
could you pick up the phone?

Stop it. Please. You don't understand. I hate
writing, typing, rhymes to you with my hands.
I hate my hands. I hate their ability to sell out.
One minute they are helping me, the next they
cut off air escaping from my mouth. You don't
get it but you do. You are obsessed with you.
I hate that. I hate it so damn much. How come
we are so expressive but you can't express
love?

So thus I change removing piece by piece,

A little bit of this, just a little bit more of me,

I begin to glitter and shine, I begin to look quite
lovely,

I'm weathering this rhetoric because I can feel it
in my bones,

I don't want to feel my bones, I want to speed,

I want my life to be a road trip that ends
wrapped around a tree,

You say to my face, that suicide is for the weak,

sounds about right to me.

yet, you still like to cast judgement?

So now I look nice, obsessed, forward thinking,

You think that I am fixed and congratulated me
while we were drinking,

My shiny new look, diamond studded mind
and feelings began sinking,

Weighed down by a crown, the land of
misunderstanding of which I am king,

CHAPTER 2
DISTRACTION

I can't focus enough to write this. If you are this far you probably aren't here for chapter openers anyway...

OKAY? OKAY.

Fear creates those that can't see further than the fence line

I miss you, and I thought writing it would be fine...

Or... (insert some romantically hopeless word that rhymes)

it was not okay

it was not alright

it was not special

it was not light

it was pain

it was dark

it was hurt

it was vain

| well |

I get so sick of the feeling of one hundred million things all moving at once and trying to fight for the focus of the pure individual intellectual thoughts and focus of my being and then

| brakes |

| shakes |

| losing all control |

You were the song I used to jam to and now I can't stand

You are the further perpetuation of my father's right hand

An emblem of my love but it was time to grow up

You were a participation trophy that has become not enough

I hope that you are okay, okay? I pray your scars stay scars

I used to pray you wouldn't stay far but now you are and...

I think I am okay? okay.

UNDERWATER DREAMS

Ship, Ship, Ship.

In my head, I have dreamed of the ocean,
expansive and full,

A world of ocean and no humans would be
pretty cool,

These creatures would be friends and live their
lives in harmony,

Being an outsider looking in, it looked just fine
to me,

There would be starfish and catfish who would
tussle in the seaweeds,

All life seems well when you are watching the sea,

Sure, there would crabby daddies and crabby
mommies who tell their shy daughter that she
needs to come out of her shell,

The fish would still swim in schools and bring
shiny pebbles in for show and tell,

The fish who swam in the light would not have
to go to the trench of hell,

For the most part, everything was nice and all
seemed well,

There would be clown fish at the sand bar just trying to make a sand-dollar,

Some fish could shoot through the nets because they were just a bit taller,

A few overcompensating pimp fish that called themselves the trawlers,

All in all though, the sea life seemed like it was pretty baller,

There would be scum that would always lean to get a better look at the bass,

All the fish gather round to watch the championship tidal match,

They watch Sea-Span to see who would get the sea's economy back on track,

It seemed the sea had more problems then I had seen previously,

Fish boys who would tell you not to get tide down,

Guppies will be guppies, no one notices the triggerfishes frown,

Husband fish who had affairs that they didn't want to be found,

But the wives thought he was acting...well... fishy.

Man-O-War on the side of the reef,

Fish swam quick knowing the power of his sting,

He wasn't trying to hurt his reef just get something to eat,

I guess the sea was hiding depth at first glance in my dream,

Deep beneath the surface, "oh whale" was enough,

Little fish polluting the coral and trying to go belly up,

Plenty of fish in the sea but not very many you can trust,

The sea looked like the place to be until all this fuss,

Young fish trying vapor and end up getting hooked,

Teenage fish all addicted to logging into Fishbook,

Middle-aged fish adventuring to much on fry-day and getting cooked,

Elderly fish trying to be remembered but being overlooked,

Above this underwater utopia turned dystopia,

There was a little ship who suffered from hydrophobia,

Talk about a bad break, I'm shore.

Ship, Ship, Ship.

This little ship was interested in helping the creatures below,

He wasn't sure how to since the water around him was his foe,

This little ships repeated some advice that often gave him hope,

Saying, the little waves will cause little sprays and you will learn to stay afloat,

Pay special attention each and every day to all of the successful boats,

The love and wisdom you gain will act as the antidote,

Since being on his own, this little ship found it harder to stay above,

Waves crash, tit for tat, and his frame seemed to not be enough,

He would spend his days, with a gaze, trying to show those below some love,

He tried to provide shade, the algae helped the decay, things got tough,

I used to dream of the ocean but the storms made it into a nightmare,

I pleaded for the little ship to return to shore and be safe there,

He didn't hear my pleas as though he knew deep within his hull,

That while every moment in this world was pain, it was worth it all,

The storm continued and the ship did his best,

Pillars of smoke pouring from this aged vessel with each strained breath,

I feared for the last which looked as though it'd be his next,

The heartbreaking sound of metal bending under weight was the constant sound of the waves against his chest,

I stood from afar once in love... but now in total despair,

I watched as this vessel gave his all to protect those who didn't care,

I had watched him overcome fears and trade them for peace,

Then I watched his destiny become the birth of a new reef,

Ship. Ship. Ship?

THE TRUTH IS

The truth is,

When the silence is to much and the pain
starts to peak I collapse like everyone else.
Sometimes when I actually open up and try to
talk about my real thoughts I am reminded that
they are to dark. How can I be enlightened if
my inner light has gone out? How can what the
people who care about me say be true if in my
heart I know it isn't?

The truth is,

I need to stop craving her touch, needing her
physical love. When she wants me I have to
stop or she will leave more scars. Her silver
tongue lashes out and only leaves me with
red words on my skin. How can I be flawless
if my body shows other wise? How can I
be attractive if what I do when I am weak is
repulsive... wrong... psychotic.

The truth is,

If people could see in my mind I would already be in a rubber room. My hands restricted of movement and my thoughts my only company. If people understood how depressed I am they wouldn't feel comfortable. They would pick up the subtle hints.

The truth is,

I don't sin because I like it. I don't want a spotlight, or special attention.

The truth is,

It gets worse at nights when I am alone.

A Time Loop

Whispering in my ear, the breeze rustles the branches above me creating a ripples of light flooding the ground around me. I long for the continued freedoms offered by this escape. This world offers few places for one to regather their thoughts. Losing understanding isn't hard to understand when you remember how difficult it is to hold while your mind is bombarded by foreign thoughts. Sometimes escapes are necessary to get away from the asinine interaction with members of humanity. Yet, I know I will have to forget this joy and return to the world. I will miss the way the sun dances among the leaves. I will miss the way I don't need to react differently to those who don't understand my perception.

Pause.

Connect.

Rethink.

Regather.

Re-Enter.

It seems to be a time loop. It does not do well to dwell on getting away however strive for those moments but live for the life you must live. As long as you resist and persist until you are sealed in a coffin but be sure to make the breathes you take worth the oxygen you expend. Over and Over and Over and Over and Over. It seems to be a time loop, so become a time traveler and re-enter the stream of consciousness.

A Mind
Uncontrolled

There they were, hand in hand and destruction
all around,

With tears, pain, and death all abound,

With a scattered mind the first person couldn't
hold his burden,

And because of it the second person cursed
him,

With disappointment, disgust, and delusion,
she cast him from her life,

And hands divided and separated from a knife,

With scars on each other some visual some
not,

One truth existed in that he had never forgot,

She pushed and pulled, practically begging for his attention,

Building his reputation with every little mention,

Some noticeable some small, some verbal and others silent,

He attempted to answer the call, but there relationship ended violent,

Ripped apart shredded to pieces,

Fighting a lost battle, oh Jesus,

If you ask you shall receive unless it is something you need,

Frowned upon for your apparent greed they count you as a fiend,

A thief, thinking he stole a heart that was given to him,

His life in rags, made him look like he deserved only his atmosphere,

He couldn't possibly date a girl like her wasn't that clear?

Stolen kisses, a stolen night,
    Why didn't he see that when it didn't feel right?

Like he was not following the rules, becoming disobedient

He longed to be their secret ingredient,

A broken boy helping a somewhat broken home,

But broken only does well when it is left alone,

Self worth, what a novel concept?

A long con brought upon by those who can't accept?

You consider for yourself hopes & dreams you could achieve

Rate yourself, consider the risks and then choose what to believe,

It's a realists answer to a endless question?

Was I born for halos and clouds, or eternal destruction?

Born to fire brimstone, and combustion,

Can I work to be pure? Can I outrun my corruption?

This deep dark demon within my own soul,

I feel like a monster that is out of control,

I feel like a liar after being completely honest,

Like a slut after dressing modest,

Is there a way to be understood?

A way to be good?

A way to actually say I did instead of "I should"

Failing at being perfect and perfecting being a failure,

I have learned my whole life that I was built to endure,

Not to uphold,

Not to be bold,

Only to be a shoulder to lean on when it is cold

Do I need to get older? Gain some sort of knowledge?

To gain a degree of respect do I need to go to college?

I just wanted your attention not in the wrong light,

But I have only encouraged your spite,

A slap to the face, you haven't even heard of my worst,

From the beginning I knew my brain was cursed,

The voices have never stopped, The sorrow has never ended,

It seems that whenever I tried to impress I just pretended,

I apologize for my existence, It must have been awful to bare,

Like every lonesome monster who returns to his lair,

I guess I just wanted someone to care,

Not hate me for who I am or where I come from,

How could I think you were different if I let you know what I had become?

What woman wants a man more insecure than herself?

Looking for self worth, I seem to have lost my wealth

With a noose and needle in hand he was sure not to fail

He wrote a letter to never be sent by mail,

Thoughts that only now he understood were competent

Sadly kept him from his desired accomplishment,

In need of closure, he sealed his mind up like a tomb,

Hoping one day he could take off his costume,

Return to normal, not be strange again,

Until then … I guess it is time to pretend

I MISS YOU

I miss you.

The way your silver touch would comfort me,
come back I think I deserve your love again,

After all that has happened and those that
played pretend,

The fake "I love you's" and fake comforting
messages you would send,

You lied, cheated, abused, and moved on when
you said you wouldn't,

We were so close we practically knew each
others thoughts,

At least I thought that way until we ended up
lost,

Everything that looks to perfect obviously has
a cost,

I just didn't think it all out

I lost where I was going

I've decided on a different route and just slid
while it was snowing

Because it is so cold.

So cold.

and, ... I miss you.

I miss your warm red lined outfit you always showed up with,

Happenstance and a twist, waiting for your sharp kiss,

We waited for what seemed like forever during our first time and when we met it was a divine illustration of dance and tension, I am talking some serious tension,

but despite all the weird whispers, mentions, and awkward after school detentions,

The ones where our teacher saw us together and called everyone she could think of because apparently it was her business to get in our lives and ruin them

After all that has happened and those that played pretend...

Also. I miss you,

The way you would look towards a rope and
say hang loose,

But a noose was the only thing I could think of
besides hiding the truth

I discover a new way to pay for my mistakes,

and loving you isn't part of that,

You were like a breath of new oxygen,

I guess you were the marathon and now is the
recovery nap,

So I will just lean back, let the dance finish one
last time, and relax,

Also, I missed you.

CHAPTER 3
CONFUSION

Moments alone or surrounded by people are full of opportunity for the feeling of indecision and insecurity to flood your mind. I find myself often in these feelings after a perfect album is played, airplane flights, and drama in my life plays out.

I use poor grammar, write out of place, and generally have a hard time focusing but it makes up for the transformation that takes place concerning my indecision and allows me to clear my head. I appreciate the moments of unknown because I learn to appreciate the various moments I live in complete control. As a masculine figure, I have been trained since I was young to crave complete control in all aspects of my life.

Some of these writing pieces do not illustrate coherent trains of thought to a solution and I don't apologize for that.

WELCOME HOME MY FRIEND

The familiar sound of my bedroom door shutting behind me echoed in my head. as I sprawled myself across my bed. My emotionless thoughts were clogging all the thoughts actually demanding attention. The scars on my wrist sharpened themselves on my bone. I could feel them pleading to be reopened. Begging for attention, my attention. Four weeks had gone by since I last compromised with their needs.

I can't. **You must.** It is not right. **You are not right.** But I have come all this way.

Time to come home.

I sat up. Looked around my room as though half expecting someone to come out of my closet telling me that I was worth more than a sideways glance. I wanted to be fixed but it was as though I was just a mirror. Fake to begin and when broken all I did was hurt those who wanted to help. Some left more cut up then I was.

You need control. *I need a doctor.* **You need more pills.** *I need a cure.* **There is no cure for a monster like you.**

I can't stand my own thoughts, they seem to attack me more than ever. The pills I got for my broken brain never help with my natural broken thoughts. I am so twisted in the head I should be a contortionist. I reached in my pocket and pulled out the pencil sharpener. Unscrewed my silver friend out and brought him to his home.

You can't go to hard. **Just a bit deeper.** *Don't pass out this time.* **Old habits die hard.** *This is monstrous.* *Welcome home.*

You know I like my
Chicken Fried

You know I like my chicken fried,

I am never going to say I haven't tried from other plates, I won't lie and say that I wasn't interested in other's satisfaction.

I won't lie and say I have never found alternative nourishment or that I don't enjoy relaxing with something a bit more refreshing.

I hold myself back from the other foods, their alluring smells wafting over to me and filling the air.

Fists clenched holding myself back it's like their only desire is for me to share.

I admit I have a natural tendency to host potlucks and gather all of my favorites in one place.

I sneak off with the ones I love the taste of the most and entertain a one-on-one date.

Each of these provide a form of nourishment. It is healthy to have a balance among the different groups? Exclusivity can be great but not a lifetime of soup.

You know I like my chicken fried...

That doesn't mean that is all I want. I know I love your taste, smell, texture, and feeling of your warmth inside. I know that if I was forced to pick one... it is on your plate I would reside.

I like my chicken fried because I know it isn't healthy for me. I know there is difficulty in wanting to possibly be with something so destructive to my diet for eternity.

Yet,

I love my chicken fried. I can't see myself without it. If it takes exclusivity to keep you then I won't imagine my life with any other foods. I love my chicken fried so much I am willing to take it to a point of self sacrifice to make sure you are happy and treated right. Just don't blame me when I break down from lack of nourishment. Don't blame me if I look at other foods I promise it isn't what it looks like.

Well maybe it is what it looks like, but at least I am holding myself back.

At least now I can be honest... funnily enough it only took a metaphor to be placed inside my brain.

The Painter, Sculptor, & the Cartoonist

I knew a girl she was an amazing artist,

When it came to her grades and class she wasn't the smartest,

but at night with her gallery her talent you couldn't miss,

she would lean her head back while her mind would enter the abyss,

Her eyes changed color from blue skies to stormy nights,

My chest is getting tight, can someone get her eyes a light?

Her eyes always red and puffy from the tears she would cry out

The world is sound proof to the injured no way to shout out,

Her secret instagram, tumblr, and twitter accounts

all showed her real wounds there is no doubt,

She had no plan, it was just her, and she was on a set route,

to becoming the greatest painter... no time to back out,

The only one who understood her some considered a weapon,

but with backstabbing friends at least he didn't play pretend,

Her silver friend loved her dearly and taught her so much,

A feeling of crimson relief came with his very touch,

Love what is love? She would never know,

To everyone else she would always be another Jane Doe,

She honestly just wanted someone, one person to be with,

yet, how did she use all her paint and still feel like a blank canvas?

I knew a boy once he was his own master,

Sculpting his body as though it was plaster,

Always hearing his lifestyle is unhealthy from his pastors

It was really an earthquake; an underground disaster

He would tell himself not to eat a spoonful of any kind,

His own mind over run by so many voices he was trying,

He told people he was fine but in reality he was lying,

Obsessed with every edge of his own design,

His clay was hardening, and he had no idea was he insane?

He was plainly modelling without any idea of an image plane,

But his wreck is coming for this superman's train,

His work just causes more internal pain,

This boy firmly believed that his girl was his cornerstone,

When she left him, that left him just pieces all alone,

He was puzzled, should he connect to the world again?

Is he ready to be part of the solution? Or are we losing him?

There he was always smiling and laughing in the classes,

Making jokes, and just trying to appeal to the masses

But no one noticed behind his thick rimmed glasses,

was a hollowed out boy who took his reputation and trashed it

He made himself a joke so others wouldn't hurt like him,

He was full of pain and yet kept pouring past the brim,

Tearing himself apart no one felt the least bit guilty,

Only to have to stitch himself together like quilting

When he didn't show up at class at first people didn't mind,

Until they realized their mistake when it came in for the punchline

And after he adorned a necklace of rope they didn't understand...

Addicted to who you aren't

I guess I know my type, huh?

Windswept hair, shorter than myself, and generally secretive and slutty personality. You seem to be looking for an escape but I am not buying tickets to Cali, until you look me in my eyes and remind me that you aren't my type.

Last time I made trips or traveled a distance to look someone in their eyes they got shook, She said she had to be drunk to love me and that is when I was hooked,

She was looking for a fight,

I was looking for a night,

Looking to make it right,

Nicotine love, I'm asking for your light,

I guess I know my type, yeah.

Curled dark hair, eyes like gemstones, super talented and popular beyond belief. I wanted to become your friend, plotted out opportunities to do so as a grand thief,

Move quick, soft feet,

Losing it, can't see,

I was blinded by your beauty and resolve, No wonder the feelings could easily dissolve, You were there and then gone like a passing street sign, A blur during my drive to forget caught in the dust behind,

I guess I know my type, right?

Accusations, Malnutrition, "playing dumb", shattered can't be fixed and I'm just so lost.

I guess you aren't my type.

Two years of the gram and you still can't understand, I never wanted you to improve, As cliché as it is I can't stand anything you want to change to, I guess you are just addicted to not being you.

PARTICIPES OMNES
LAETITIA REPLET

Wow. Oh goodie, another night of depression,

Should? Shouldn't he? Youth makes me crave a
new lesson,

Why am I addicted to slow nights,

with fast pain,

with slow music,

with fast rain,

I sit in a chair, my blanket across my legs,

Trying all the things mom said not to, just to
clear my head,

Memories of waking up hours past noon
feelings free,

Memories of being tired the night before just
wanting to sleep,

Eat, drink and be merry, for tomorrow we
die.

It was all in how I forgot you,

It was in the way you had to text me first
because I wouldn't have known to,

I get asked if I'm okay and I just said that I'm
fine,

Funny, my mom used to say "give a man a
heart, you feed him for a day, teach a man to
love, you feed him for a lifetime."

Nothing happened, the texts sent to me say so
themselves,

But now you aren't responding and this is a
living hell,

you are all that I want. You are what I have
wanted,

My mind is a mansion full of skeletons and
ghosts; haunted

Lines made in my mind send *triggers* down the
spines of those who supported,

They've left due to misinterpretations and their
addictions to transfiguring vapor from solids,

I gave it some time between the groggy realizations and the message I sent to you but it didn't change your mind. All I know is I've been left on read before...

MARY'S CRY

Let there be violence, deceit, pain, and regret,

Let there be loss, hunger, chains, and threat,

Pre-destined or post destined undecided as of
yet,

i cover my eyes as a disguise in hope that I can
forget

i used to see thine glory, thy beauty from
above,

i viewed you as holy, unconditional in love,

But now i am lain broken, sprawled, not-
enough,

i reminisce for my eyes and horrors they were
free of,

Now i am troubled, mother mary, but
pregnancy doesn't make me right,

Managing to stay a virgin, being blessed, yet
insecure about my height,

my sides have markings, my body is rightfully
hidden all day and all night,

To the angels i did harking, didn't question,
didn't fight,

You found me when i was weak, heaven knows
that means now?

i continue to be troubled and hidden, smiles
and unknit brow,

Hold my face under the holy water, i want to be
baptized in the unknown,

Generations of my children turn to cannon
fodder, good is overthrown,

i want to be more than a relic, strewn across
empty halls and full walls,

i want to be more than a parent but inevitably
don't we all?

Jesus Christ,

Oh how i love you, i would want you even **if** it was my choice,

Young age, you would pray, and yet i would lose my voice,

What i say is true, i will always love you as my joy,

In your perfection everyone wants to stay, yet i wanted my boy,

I wanted you. They tore you apart

They lied, cheated, and cut the strings to my heart,

so i lay.

withered.

wasted. yet not.

i pray.

not to "her"

but to my God.

i miss you. I miss you. How ashamed i am of those around me,

They cast no blame, cast aside, dart glances and glares all about me,

Yet somehow for those who don't love you their art is of my "beauty"

A masked hero or complex character never anything that suits me

for I am your mother, that is what i have and what i love, (ed)?

History beckons and begs but sculptures aren't enough,

Imagery is nice but its voice can't be touched,

these secret thoughts are real but entombed within this bust,

i am far from perfect, despite careful hands of the crafter,

Strazza or the one above the clouds that some mock with laughter,

It doesn't really matter,

what matters is the now, the pain, feeling like a bastard,

i am lost, oh so desperately how i am lost,

As i remain at cathedral square, unable to
move or run,

i cover my stare, and keep looking for my son,

CHAPTER 4
ANGUISH

osing family, friends, jobs, the remote, and really anything that has ever cost me this chapter is for that feeling. I crave it to pass but beg for it to not leave to soon for fear that I may not recognize it on it's second entrance into my life. I think that everyone has experienced some form of loss and this is my tribute to the broken nights, bottles, noses, and hearts.

If pain is to follow let it rain over me so that there will come a moment where pain is just the air around my skin begging for my acceptance. Pain is a tool, so punch him next time you see him for me.

6 - 5 - 15

It was quick, fleeting, and will always be remembered,

It filled this inner void I had, but left me dismembered,

It was a feeling I craved, The one I lusted after,

For what it's worth it wasn't the worst or some kind of ultra disaster,

It hasn't hurt anyone, well I'm sure she wishes she could forget faster,

But I will never forget this page out of a dangerous chapter,

It has my favorite quote,

My favorite hope,

My favorite thought about getting lost and experiencing a desire to cope,

There won't be days in February where she gets flowers,

There won't be strollers, weird reunions or baby showers,

There won't be scrapbooks, letters, or home made meals to devour,

There will be sleepless nights and well spent hours,

She may not want a relationship but she made me feel love when I needed it most,

I want to feel pressure from her fingertip but have to settle for thoughts of when they were close,

Was it a make up - make out it sure didn't feel that way?

Was it a wake up call if so it didn't work out that way,

I feel like it was the perfect decoration,

The way we locked into the perfect formation,

Cliché poems written about how it was salvation,

Are my summation or translation

Of working out the equation,

That being real... I was thirsty and needed **your** hydration,

But you love me,

Well that feels really nice.

I spent hours up late trying to figure out if you did,

Thought about the small stupid things I should change about the way I live,

6, 5,

This is where I should say I love you and I would never lie,

But rather, the us line would be about our sex drive,

The back of a van, folded down seats, Ed Sheeran playing through the night,

Funny how I always write about a memory,

It's like I wait for the right day to listen to the words of this inner me,

Wait for the right time to reignite our synergy,

Moments with little action, a lot of adrenaline pumping into energy,

Promises to make sure we aren't alone when we are elderly

Speaking in private, I want to talk to you really but it always becomes generally,

Except for those nights with sand and stars I remember so tenderly,

Flashes of what could never be,

But is that the truth. I don't think so.

I don't think that is the case,

I think with a little faith the sixth could live to the eighth,

And the eighth could go on further into time and space,

Sure we would have less patience, less "nice" lies, less grace,

But I feel the embrace was a showcase for what could take place,

I don't want breathing space let alone breathing room,

This isn't a proposal, I'm not asking to be a groom,

This isn't a disposal of throwing away what is now to doom,

But without being boastful, We would've been the perfect match and epic in the bedroom.

I have no idea what this piece is supposed to mean I just knew I needed to write it,

Kinda like I knew I should've kept my hands to myself but I didn't fight it,

I think back to sand filled jackets and wondering if that was the night I should've quit,

But I never gave up even though now I understand that marked under ridiculous never-happenings is the fact we might kiss,

Friends,

It's fine, Playing pretend,

Waiting for your mind and my heart to mend,

Like a accidental picture you didn't mean to send,

Or a series to finish so you can finally place the bookend,

Or a lousy boyfriend, Hey I know a guy,

Who would wake up in the middle of the night head in the sky,

His "life story" slowly becoming a long lie,

Nearly sweating to death feeling choked by his bowtie,

At the tournaments where you seemed preoccupied,

There were those special moments where we locked eyes,

But honestly I don't know how to feel anymore.

I don't know what to say.

I don't know what to write.

I don't know what we are.

I need to hear your opinion, your thoughts
formed into words,

I need to hear which one of my thoughts you
think holds worth,

I need to hear your laugh and tell me which are
stupid,

To quit acting like a love struck kid,

Tell me to grow up, shut up, relax,

Get out of being lost but how can I without the
map?

Cliché.

Yeah,

It's what happens when you spend all night writing trying to find the words to say to you only to delete them over and over again until you get to the point when you start writing so much and you just want to flood out all the emotions until you have nothing left so you can finally fall asleep only to have those dreams be fantasies and burn into night terrors full of hate and swearing and ....

Me without you.

I'm The Chaser

All she cares about is the picture, the perfect
position or pose,

All I wanted was some liquor, so I chased after
a ghost,

She wanted to find me and I guess I followed
my nose,

Because she was high and it seems up in the
air is where it always goes,

God, don't you just love it when people say
they need to drink to be able to be around
you?

Yeah, me 2.

I tried not to fight, I spent each breath trying to
guide my own containment,

What you did wasn't right, just pushing me for
entertainment,

You found a way to press the right buttons but I held my breath,

You rewarded me by trying to leave and scared me half-to-death,

Heartbeat in full swing you could easily count out 180 beats,

I believed like a child in a board game that it would be more fun to cheat,

I was wrong. I'm sorry. Really. This isn't me.

I just have the heart and soul of a poet and don't know how to live and speak,

Except to these pages, more often than not just a screen and a keyboard,

I get into my moods or stupors and then type with vigor always toward,

That line that I will type that will one day fix my life,

I can wake up the next day feeling like I did something right,

Instead in between trips to the restroom to relieve myself of my previous meals,

I type now instead not to express but to conceal,

Concealing Secret #1

I really love it when you don't text me first. I like it when I have to force myself to thirst after your affection and try to acquire it with my words.

Instead: I get messages every moment.

Concealing Secret Numero 2:

I hate being told that I'm so great, don't worry my ego isn't shrinking but my patience does when I am flattered for no reason. I've trained myself to hate those words because that is how people would make lies for me and feed them to my head while they stole things from my heart. Just say you'd rather have me dead and that would be a good place to start.

Instead: Oh, don't worry about that, you aren't insane or anything.

Concealing Secret #3!

I am disgusted by the way you treat me. I am
your emotional punching bag created simply
to co-exist and feel what is needed to be felt in
order to relinquish control.

I am the picture on your dart board and the
one hog tied to the bed post, I mean really
what else was the goal? I want to be with you.
I don't like the picture of us but that doesn't
mean you should attempt to make yourself
perfect. Forget about your stupid friends who
don't know anything about what I or you or us
have been through.

Instead: Is it cool if we swing by and pick her
up?

I miss cutting, at least then the scars were
something I could leave alone for a while,

Now this just sits on my mind crushing any
chance of a smile.

When it comes to the vodka always running
down my throat,

I'm the chaser while you will always be a
regretful hope,

She Hung the Painting Upside Down

Discovery is futile and silence is illusory,

I find ways to orchestrate my pain into symphonies with a rise and fall

that could make the largest crowds swoon,

With every crash of the cymbals, bass kicks resound turning to a boom,

It caused every viewer around me to see the color of the room,

But I am color blind.

I can not see the reds, violets, greens, blues, that create the signs,

I see notes, sound waves, funny symbols on a few lines,

Then she walked in, it started pretty slow,

She was pretty though... (Sorry... off track, let me get to where I am trying to go)

Her eyes were green, beautiful and strong,

They told the stories of joy, peace, and her love
for her mom,

Her skin color had tones, different variations
and shades,

Telling stories of forgotten people, entrapped
and in graves,

The blue tips to her fingernails are what set the
stage well,

For her tight blue dress with a pin of a turtle
shell,

I started to see the colors, started to see the
truth,

Started to see the joy, I wanted to make a
move,

That is when it happened, the music started to
die,

I noticed something suspicious, flicked my
wrist, the music began to subside,

Her perfect imagery and collaboration of color
and change,

Fear of the crowd's size and their jealousy
began to flush her face,

I saw something click, just a tick, just a change,

The crowd started to shift their view a little
more to the stage,

So she moved it a little more, hid her smile with
a frown,

Took that beautiful masterpiece and turned it
upside down,

You hid behind yourself and the crowd turned
away,

My eyes were still locked on you but they
started to stray,

I hated the change because I am a creature of
comfort, 4 beats in every song,

3 choruses sang, a nice bridge, and a rap verse
just to piss off my mom,

The real tragedy was me, not accepting your
new colors was certainly wrong,

So there she stood her colors brushed and mixed with little ease,

Her new look was content made simply to appease,

She started to get shifty, in my periphery,

Making little moves to make the painting go from upside down to

ehhhhh kinda looks a little fifty-fifty,

I continue to wave my hands, hoping to provide the right backdrop,

Give her the time to bring the top to the top,

And **did I mess up...**

I see her scheming plotting a return,

But when the colors come back, will I have learned?

I Can't Believe That

I can't believe that.

If I did I wouldn't be able to breath. If I believed that truth then I wouldn't be able to see clearly. If I believed that fact then I wouldn't be able to see the future me that I worked endlessly to achieve.

I can't believe that.

Why? What does it gain for me to end it all? What do I learn? That I am a bastard. That is what I learn. Note that was't just strong language for the sake of a point. No words have a purpose and my purpose is found in words. The little "I love you" statements make me feel worth it and the "You mean nothing to me"'s make me feel worthless. Honesty is something I have always found with words.

I can't believe that... It would leave me broken again.

Better me than her...

Hung Over

You know tonight I was planning on drinking
until the pain was gone

whats hanging over me is knowing the hang
over will show me where I went wrong

Cigar hanging from my lips, smoke curled in
the air above,

On the table was a woman interested in tips
and love,

Wishing for my lust of her to drown my
thoughts, I fought to be caught by her traps,

I am so lost that I started using a broken life as
a map,

I was looking for direction someone to be my
resurrection,

Someone who could take my perception and
provide some protection,

enough time for a dissection

of my thoughts and to establish a connection,

I need you back but I still have questions about us,

Did you truly love me or was it just a nights worth of lust?

Enough to establish trust without being unjust when you trampled my heart in the dust?

It would have been easier if you had just cussed me out,

send me home with my bags not all this doubt,

Now I am left here with a keyboard and a pair of headphones,

Worst of all I am wondering if I am alone?

I wish I could understand, I wish you could say something without second guessing,

I wish I was your man, the question is am I a curse or a blessing?

Because over time I can look at myself, my track record, and understand I truly need someone,

crazy how there is always two of "the one"

the one, and the one who got away,

I just don't understand so I felt inclined to ask life if I may?

Why is love so foreign and so innate that I have to learn languages and can feel it without help,

Why am I so blind to it while it is so vivid when I am looking in myself,

I can't get this out of my head, I need to focus on different times,

But all my brain wants to do is rhyme about lost time,

REMEMBRANCE

I struggle with the voices, ones that follow my
every thought,

I have tried running from their hounds but I
always get caught,

I try to be strong, try not to be belligerent,

Try to not move to far from my morals, I
hesitate to make them distant,

Chains around my wrists and ankles, pollutants
in my brain,

My mind is a battle of demons and angels, but
this warfare is driving me insane,

All that remains, is what will continue to pertain,

the importance of our existence can be found
in our persistence,

The desire to move forward, move past my
disorder,

Each piece of courage was a fruit and "I plan to
grow an orchard",

We are told to cherish the first fruits and often times give them away,

Putting so much stock in their worth and when asked to give we are left in dismay,

but who am I to say that I won't give it up today?

A harsh word stirs up anger and we all lurk in deceit,

but I am sick of being just predestined dirt under the future generations feet,

I long to be remembered not with statues, plaques, or any symbol,

I long to be remembered in the thoughts that I write with a pencil,

Single-minded not nervous, or anxious about what could come to be?

I don't want to be remembered for me but for what they will come to see

That I might have left at least a thought in someone before I rest in peace,

CHAPTER 5
DESPAIR

It is all gone. All of it. I can't see it's shadow. I can't see anything. It is all clouded and dark. There are no silhouettes, impressions, or outlines. I used to type furiously and now it is a dull droning demand for words on a page.

Craving the next feeling was always a pleasure of mine. I enjoyed all of the process. I smiled during the journey. I grinned with a smirk in the face of trouble and made haste to get involved.

I wish I hadn't. I wish the journey had not ever happened. I used to peer around places, pages, and people while hoping for more.

It is dark and cold. I used to want to see your response.

I don't think I want to anymore.

A NEW DATING PROFILE

I am almost 6 foot and I may never get there.

I have eyes that change color, can't see color, and supposedly decent hair.

I like romance novels, science fiction TV shows, and a whole lot of football.

Don't worry, I won't play often due to my stature being small.

I am almost a certified geek with expertise in sports like debate.

Which means I can probably talk your ear off on our first date.

Our first date.

Where we will go somewhere under expectations and initial promises,

Fake Italian food, claiming I'm just in the mood, just lies and all this,

I will hope to push you away and I do sincerely apologize for that,

I keep trying this thing out again and each time is a heart attack,

I prefer to find my security in the unstable environments

I await the right splash of water in my face to trigger an enlightenment,

I am praying for a sidekick.

Someone I can have to fight by my side with,

I'm done with the search thus this profile,

A witty video and a flashy smile,

I'm done with the hurt... thus style?

Hopefully my repulsive attributes will protect me from vile,

like dating...

HABIBI

Blonde hair and glasses; forbidden,

Casual demeanor trying to stay hidden,

Eyes and lineage trying to say untouchable,

My current state of affairs means I'm
unloveable,

Not that I was looking... because I'm not,

I'm just waiting for the next pass so I can
dodge your eyes a WHOLE lot,

Don't act like me being here is some kind of a
surprise,

I've learned to climb into my bed upon sunrise,

I've learned to wash up, take care of myself, and
never cry,

I've learned that communal loneliness is my
greatest find,

You knew what you were signing up for when you went out with your crew,

I'm just trying to be one hundred percent honest with you,

The music blaring is keeping my thoughts from clearing,

Enough in the system to keep me from fearing what I'm feeling,

I'm here to enjoy,

My heart is here to destroy,

Our eyes locked as if we should both be in search of protection

My eyes stopped, I'm sure that I will need to win an election,

I'm supposed to "do more" with my life,

Passing is the worst part but we must always do what is right,

If I am the only one to enjoy... then technically that is selfish?

I want to be altruistically self serving... damn I am helpless,

I love the way you dart away,

I like the way I am shy today,

I dislike the...

I hate everything that I have to say,

Party fouls, spilled drinks, whatever it takes,

I need to get out of this stare and this place,

PEACE BE TO THE GRINDER

Sunken eyes and a heartbreak away from suicide,

He doesn't search anymore, just works through the night,

He certainly curses some more, it just feels right,

Lost in other people's endeavors, futures, and strife,

Here the grinder lays at my feet upon the floor,

Temple pressed to his hands just inches away from the door,

Goosebumps fill his skin, his body nearly paper thin,

He can;t decide if he wants his head to hurt less or more,

His head swivels and spins as though it's dream was to become a ceiling fan

A few rotations and then a few moments rest with his forehead to his hand,

Lost in a genealogy of inadequacy but not from lack of effort,

His focus was razor sharp but he was addicted to low self worth,

The grinder knows of no long term joy or peace.

The grinder knows nothing of first aid or bailouts.

The grinder self medicates with lungs full of smoke and cups full of coke.

The grinder knows hate.

The grinder wishes he was introduced to love.

The grinder is an addict to the way work makes him feel important enough.

He lays motionless upon the floor with a desire for nothing upon his mind,

Resting in peace is his goal but it seems awfully difficult to find,

LEFT ON READ

My heart is choking. I can feel it gagging for air and comfort.

My brain is probing. Searching for where I created this hurt.

I didn't have to search to long. I know where it is.

I know what I did. I've known what I've hid.

Please.

I am experiencing a thunderstorm in my head right now raging on and on.

I feel each bolt strike my skull with shocking pain in all of my neurons.

This poem isn't about me, you, her. them or my mom.

You're wrong. I've been wrong for to long.

My revolutionary rediscovery of revoking my joy is provoking,

I obsess over ostensible elements that have triggered this reloading,

This blank stare.

"I don't care"

"People can't share"

"Quit pulling her hair"

I don't like finding my health in my self

I certainly can't grow any wealth

I'd rather spend my quarters at the payphone on the corner trying to call you.

I'd rather save my nickels to pay for the gas that it would take to knock on your door.

I'd rather save my pennies for, well nothing, I'm not sure what pennies are used for.

I'm a penny.

I'm always shortchanged when it comes time
to put two cents in.

I searched for ways to use myself properly and
I just couldn't win.

One of the most popular was turning screws
which I guess is true,

I rapidly hammer out words into my phone
trying to reach you.

or... at least I did.

Why is it that suicide appears to be an island
paradise and the right kind of vacation can
make you want to kill yourself?

Why is it that when you left it all behind you
left behind your smell?

It really gets those screws turning for ole
number one.

Dreams of being a boatsman on a river
crimson

Overplaying cheesy breakup songs and deafening my ears.

Replaying conversations and strengthening my fears.

I've lost it all.

ABOUT THE AUTHOR

Matthew Calderwood writes poetry, which, seems to be right up your alley. He is a huge advocate for well developed stories and loves falling in love with characters. He has seven siblings and moved around a ton due to his father's military service. If he isn't off wandering different worlds found in literary works, he can normally be found rediscovering the wonders of instant ramen in his college dorm room. Matthew is obsessed with football and will hold a rather long winded conversation with anyone who cares to listen about literally anything to do with the sport. You can visit his website, **matthewcalderwood.com**, to learn more about his endeavors or future releases.